I0087016

How to Play Basketball: A Guide to Getting Better By Playing Pick-up Games

By Thomas Wilkins

Hoops Education, 2012

Table of Contents

About Me...................Page 3

Introduction...............Page 6

Goal Setting..............Page 10

Part 1: Fitness...........Page 14

Part 2: Fundamentals..Page 19

Part 3: Skills..............Page 29

Conclusion...............Page 44

Review...................Page 46

Hoops Education, 2012

About Me

My mission is to help people live T.he S.marter W.ay. Through Hoops Education I can share the knowledge, secrets and advice to players and coaches that will help them become smarter, better, and ultimately more effective. My vision is to give players and coaches the best information so that they can improve their skill sets.

When it comes to basketball, I have been involved in just about every aspect imaginable. Through a lot of hard work and a handful of lucky breaks I was able to live out one of my dreams of playing Division 1 basketball. One of my most well-known accomplishments was walking on at the University of North Carolina-Chapel Hill and playing for the Tarheels during the 2005-2006 season. During that season we went 23-8 and made a 2nd round NCAA Tournament appearance. I also started at point guard for the Junior Varsity basketball team at UNC from 2002-2004. During my tenure as a Tarheel I played for Roy Williams (Head Basketball Coach at UNC/College Basketball Hall of Fame/Basketball Hall of Fame), Jerod Haase (Assistant Basketball Coach at UNC) and Doug Wojick (Head Basketball Coach at the University of Tulsa). I also played against numerous McDonald's High School All-Americans, Final Four MVPs, a Naismith Award Winner, 3 AP-All Americans, a Bob Cousy Award Winner, 1st and 2nd Round NBA Draft Picks, NBA players and other phenomenal basketball players. I was fortunate enough to coach with Mickey Bissette at Green Hope High School (4A classification) in Morrisville, NC off and on from 2002-2007 where we made 2 state playoff appearances and had 3 Division 1 players. I also coached an AAU team the Apex Force from 2005-2007 where we made appearances in 2 AAU National Championships, the Charlie Weber Invitational and the AAU Super Showcase in Orlando, FL. We also were ranked in the top 5 in our state during that time, won the North Carolina 17-U State Games Championship and the North Carolina USBA State Championship. I have also coached at the Roy Williams Basketball Camp, Herb Sendek Team Basketball Camp, Stanford University Basketball Camp, Elevate Basketball Clinics with Keith Moore (Assistant Basketball Coach at Iowa State University) among other camps and clinics. I have been very fortunate to be around some great players, coaches and people in the game of basketball.

My goal with Hoops Education is to share this knowledge with other players and coaches to help them develop into the best person they can be and ultimately help them achieve their goals inside and outside the game of basketball. Thank you for taking the time to share your journey with me, it will be a fun ride!

I'm out!
Thomas Wilkins

Introduction

I now know the reason I was not improving to the level of a top player in the nation. I did not have a focus when I was on the court.

Hoops Education, 2012

Hello Hooper!

Practice makes perfect is what they always say right? What happens if you are always practicing the wrong things? What happens if you are practicing the right things but the wrong way? If you are practicing the wrong things or practicing the wrong way you are not going to be a perfect player. Never mind perfect, you will not even be a good player. I definitely agreed with Vince Lombardi when he said, "Only perfect practice makes perfect". If you are trying to become the best basketball player you can be then you need to make sure you are working on the right things in the right ways. This guide is designed to help you work on the right things so you can elevate your game! If you take these principles and apply them to your pick-up games you will be a Hooper!

When I think back to the amount of time I spent on the basketball court per day it is inexcusable that I did not become a better player. I was playing basketball for 4 or 5 hours a day. I was constantly shooting at my hoop in the yard or on a court trying to get a couple Ws. I often ask myself how I did not develop into a top 100 player in the nation. It had nothing to do with my team or where I lived or my physical ability. You have to know that no matter the obstacle the only thing stopping you from overcoming that obstacle is your will power. Your perseverance will carry you through any barrier to your goals. Seriously, I was not gaining as much as I could from those countless hours with a round, orange ball in my hand. I now know the reason I was not improving to the level of a top player in the nation. I did not have a focus when I was on the court. I was not focused on building good habits. I wanted to put the ball between somebody's legs or make the people watching the game "ohhhh" and "ahhhh". I wanted to hit somebody with that nasty crossover that made them topple to the ground. Do not be this person! Do not allow yourself to go play pick-up games and only pick up bad habits.

I am not just writing this to you. I am writing this to the younger me in hopes that somebody in a time machine will pick up this book, hand it to the young Thomas and it will change my future. Since the chances of that happening are slim I guess I am mostly writing this for you. The tips I provide here are not solely intended to be read. I know they are written in a guide but they are not intended to read and then thrown aside. These tips are meant to be implemented so you can turn into a better, smarter player. So you can become a Hooper! As you are reading this book you should be thinking, "how can I use this to become better?"

Let us get to it!

Goal Setting

If you are not committed to implementing something from each section and then monitoring your performance you might as well stop reading this guide right now.

Most things you do in life should involve setting and working towards goals. When you go to play pick-up you should have some goals that you always set for yourself. I have outlined 3 areas that you should always have in mind.

The 3 areas I have outlined are:
1. Fitness
2. Fundamentals
3. Skills

Each area builds on the area that came before it. To use the material in this guide effectively it will be required that you set goals in each one of these areas and monitor your performance. If you are not committed to implementing something from each section and then monitoring your performance you might as well stop reading this guide right now.

These 3 areas were selected for specific reasons and they are in a specific order. You cannot do anything well if you are out of shape. Hence the reason I put fitness first. You might already be talented, but if you are out of shape your talent will decline as your fatigue increases. If you are always pushing yourself to improve your fitness level you will find that the rest of your game will improve as well. Not only will you improve, you will be able to perform at a high level consistently. Some players are great in the first game but after that they become below average because they are so out of shape. If you push yourself to reach your fitness goals you will find yourself in a better position to improve.

The fundamentals are so important because they are the basic building blocks of your skills. If you do not learn the fundamentals then you cannot develop a high skill level. I have not outlined all the fundamentals in the game of basketball but I did highlight the ones that will give you the best opportunity to succeed. If your goals are to make it to the next level then you will have to be fundamentally sound. I know the professional athletes look like they just run and jump, but they have the fundamentals down!

The skills portion is designed to help you become a great player. These skills will make you a Hooper! The skills are some combination of everything that comes before it and then taking it to the next level. A lot of the skills will involve using your brain to get ahead of your opponent. Every sport has a mental aspect to it, these tips will help you master the mental aspect of the game.

Part 1: Fitness

You are building habits when you are playing pick-up games. If you play a pick-up game in a lazy manner guess what?

When you are going to play pick-up the idea should be to get into game shape. This is an opportunity for you to practice all the things you have been working on individually. You want this pick-up game experience to be as close to a real game as possible for you. You want to make sure that you are playing as hard as you can all the time. You are building habits when you are playing pick-up games. If you play a pick-up game in a lazy manner guess what? That habit of laziness will spill into your real game. You also never know who is watching you. You do not ever want to be labeled as the lazy player. That lazy label is hard to come back from Hoopers. So here are some tips you can use to ensure that you are getting the fitness aspect from the pick-up games:

1)Run!

This one is so simple! I cannot tell you how many times I see people just waiting on one end of the court or another. How are you going to get better if you are never in a play? You need to make sure that when that rebound is secured or that ball is scored you are hustling to the other end. I have heard plenty of coaches say that the race down the court is won in the first 2 steps. Think about that for a second. The person who gets down to the other end first is not the fastest person. It is the person who takes the first 2 steps the fastest. Make sure you take those 2 steps before anybody else does! For post players it is important to beat your man down the court so you can get good post position. If your guard has their head up you might even get an easy layup because your defender is still trying to take their first 2 steps. For guards it is important to push the ball up the court because you might find a teammate wide open or get an easy layup while everybody else is admiring the wrong baseline. I cannot tell you how many easy points I have manufactured just by running the court. I can also tell you that I have made many plays just by sprinting back on defense. You should be running all the time because basketball is played at a fast pace. If you want a lot of stops in play then you should try football, they huddle after every down.

2)Sit Down!

When you are on defense you need to sit down in a defensive stance. My college coaches would light into us if they were looking at video and you were standing on defense.

When you are standing up on defense that tells a coach you are not ready to play. You might as well untie your shoes too! In most sports that involve quick, explosive moves you will hear coaches talk about being in an athletic position. You will only be able to make a play on defense if you are in an athletic position. You just want to be sure you have your knees bent and you are always paying attention to the ball and your man. If your knees are bent and you are in position to make a play you will make more plays. In football they talk a lot about defenders being in position to make a play. I know it is as important in basketball to be in the right place. The first step to being in position is being in a stance. This is hard to do and let me tell you it will burn. Ultimately you will build the muscle in your legs to the point where this does not bother you. At first it is tough but if you want to be a Hooper you have to be excited about doing the tough things!

3)Warm up/Cool down

When that first game starts you should already be sweating. You want to make sure your muscles are loose because if they are not warmed up it could lead to injury. No matter how many things you work to improve, if you are not healthy you cannot play. Avoiding injuries is as simple as taking care of your body. If you go out there and try to go full speed without properly getting loose then you are sending your body into shock. Your body is confused because it was moving at a nice pace not sweating and now you want it to be at peak performance. Even your best race cars cannot reach their top speeds in 3 seconds, so why would your body be able to do that? Be sure to take 10 to 15 minutes to do a light jog, do some dynamic stretching and get some shots up. If you do this correctly you will be ready to play once they check the ball to start the game.

When the game finishes just be sure to get a nice stretch in afterwards. Usually people sit around taking off all of their gear anyway so take 10 or 15 minutes to stretch before you leave. The cool down should include more basic, static stretches that do not involve a lot of movement.

Part 2: Fundamentals

These fundamentals are vital to your success as a basketball player. Guess what college coaches want to see?

Fundamentals? Wait you mean to tell me that I am writing about becoming a better player and I am starting with the stuff they teach in first grade? Everybody knows these things right? What kind of advanced training begins with the basics that everybody already knows? Well if everybody at one point knew this information they have since forgotten it. These fundamentals are vital to your success as a basketball player. Guess what college coaches want to see? They do not want to see a player that cannot stick to the basics. As a coach it was always easier to work with players who could use the fundamentals during game play. If you are always working on the basics they will soon become part of your routine. Once these basics become part of your routine you will be prepared to do some of the more difficult things. I would say concentrate on one of these things each time you play. I have divided them by offense and defense. Once you get the hang of one of the fundamentals build by working on the others one at a time. Eventually it will become part of your game then you are ready to take your game to the next level.

Defense

1)Box out

Controlling the backboard is one of the biggest keys to any game. If you can positively contribute to the rebounding battle you are putting yourself in a good position to win. When you see a shot go up you need to find the person you were guarding and box them out. Simple concept here is Hit-Pin-Spin-Grip. First you want to find the person you were guarding. Next you want to put your forearm somewhere in their midsection to keep them in that spot. Then you want to spin so you have them on your back. Finally you want to go after the rebound with two hands.

2)Challenge shots

So you have done everything in your power to make sure your man did not catch the ball easily and you slid your feet so you are in good position. Even when you are in good position people will still get shots up. As long as you put a hand up you have done your job. So the key here is stay on the ground. I do not care how many pump fakes they make you stay down. All you want to do is get a hand up to contest the shot. Where you put that hand is up to you. I have seen defenders put the hand in the shooters face. This is not my preference because honestly when I shoot I do not even see that little hand in my face. My preference would be to put your hand near the ball. If your hand is near the ball and your feet are on the ground then you put yourself in great position to contest the shot and box out.

Please pay special attention to the fact this is CHALLENGING SHOTS not blocking shots. Being a shot blocker is a special skill learned over time, challenging shots is something anybody can do no matter their skill level.

3)Slide your feet

I know we all want to pluck that crossover. As a guard every time I see somebody dribble I am thinking steal. In a real game you will most likely be called for a reaching foul. Again this is about building good habits that will translate into a real game. You want make sure that you are sliding along with the offensive player and that you stay in between them and the basket. Your goal should be to keep them in front of you. This is not just for the perimeter players. If you are guarding somebody in the post you want to do the same thing by sliding your feet to stay between him and the basket. If the offensive player gets in between you and the basket they win!

4)Get to the midline

This is one of the most important defensive principles you will ever learn. Let's imagine there is a line from the front of the rim on one end to the front of the rim on the other end. That line would split the court in half vertically. That is what we call the midline. Should you find yourself on the right side of the court and the ball is on the left side of the court you should have one foot on the midline. This principle will put you in a good position to help on the drive. The hard part about being on the midline is being able to follow the person you are guarding too. It will take mental focus to be able to see ball and man, especially as those things change positions. All of the good defensive teams I was a part of lived and died by getting to that midline. It takes hard work but as you start to clog up the middle it will make it very difficult for opposing teams to get easy baskets. Coaches

Hoops Education, 2012

are always looking for great team defenders. I would take 5 guys that work together to shut down an opposing team all day every day. Work like crazy to get your foot on that midline when the ball is on the opposite side. This is really tough but once you start to do it you will notice you are in better position on defense.

5)Get through screens

You have to fight your way through every single pick that the opposing team tries to set on you. Depending on the type of screen you are facing you will want to do different things. Unless it is a shooter you want to find a way to be in between your man and the ball. If you are getting to the midline then this will make getting through screens pretty easy. If you happen to be guarding a shooter you want to make sure you follow in their footsteps or shadow them so you can be ready to challenge their shot. When you are playing pick-up it is easy to develop the habit of holding people or pulling their shirt, do not fall victim to this bad habit! When you have to foul somebody to stop them, guess what? You are not stopping them! If it was a real game you would be on the bench because you would be in foul trouble. Stop being lazy and guard your person the right way!

Offense

6)Use screens

This is pretty simple if you want to score you have to learn how to use screens. For post players you want to use screens to find a place in the paint to park yourself. For shooters you want to find a way to get some daylight between you and your defender so you can knockdown your jumpers. Slashers you want to be able to use a ball screen to penetrate into the paint so you can finish at the rim. The first thing you want to do is set up the screen by taking a step away from the screen. Next you want to do a good job of not allowing any room between your screener's outside shoulder and your inside shoulder. Then you want to be sure to explode around the screen so the defenders have to make a split second decision. If you use screens properly there is very little a defense can do to stop you and your teammates.

7)Follow your shot

Players who can get extra possessions are basketball gold! When you put up a shot you should have a general idea about where that ball is going. If you suspect that shot is not going in you should sprint to where you believe it will fall and grab it. In any game of basketball the team that defends and rebounds usually wins. When you can grab offensive rebounds it will give your team another chance to score. Offensive rebounds also kill the morale of the defense because now they have to guard you again. This principle is often forgotten but if you start to get easy put backs you are not only getting easy buckets, you are building a great habit. Big guys especially should be doing this. Usually if you are one of the biggest people on the court then guess what? You have the best chance of rebounding the ball if comes off the rim. Use your body to your advantage and you will become a rebounding machine.

8)Get in triple threat

Every single time you catch the ball you should be in a triple threat position. A triple threat position means you are in a position to pass, shoot or drive. You get in that position by catching the ball and getting into an athletic stance. If you are on the perimeter you immediately want to face the basket. If you are in the post your back may be to the basket and then you just want to get into an athletic position. In either case you should have two hands on the ball, your knees bent and balanced. If you are in an athletic position before your defender is then it puts you at an advantage. If you watch any great scorer it is often what they do before they ever put the ball on the deck that allows them to consistently beat their defender.

9)Set screens

I know it is pick-up and I know that people want to prove they can beat the person in front of them one on one. I get that. As competition gets better it will be nearly impossible to beat people one on one because organized teams play team defense. If the defense is working together doesn't it just make sense that the offense would do the same? If you want to be a good teammate you will have to set screens for your teammates. When the ball gets checked it is simple to set a down screen for a teammate.

Hoops Education, 2012

Do not be the selfish player that just sets ball screens. When you set good screens 2 things happen: you get your teammate open and you will be more open. If you are making the defense work by setting a good screen your defender will most likely have to help. When your defender helps guess who will be open? You got it. You are open! So get your feet set, have your shoulders facing the direction you want your teammate to go and be ready to catch the ball if you are open due to your defender helping.

Part 3: Skill

Now that the foundation has been laid, let's look at 5 skills you can develop while playing pick-up games.

Hoops Education, 2012

Alright so you have been working on improving your fitness by running the court, staying in your stance, warming up and cooling down. You have been working on your defensive fundamentals by boxing out, challenging shots, sliding your feet, getting to the midline and getting through screens. You have been working on your offensive fundamentals by using screens, following your shots, using the triple threat position and setting screens. You should feel good about what you have accomplished because you are now truly on your way to becoming a better basketball player. Now that the foundation has been laid, let's look at 5 skills you can develop while playing pick-up games.

1) Become a stopper: Put the handcuffs on your opponent

When you go to the court you should always want to be the best person there. That really starts with becoming a defensive stopper. First you want to guard the best person on the other team. Find a challenge so you can get better. When you stand across from a player and say "I got them" that means that you are going to make them work. In no way, shape or form should it be easy for the person you are guarding to score. In order for you to become a defensive stopper and put the "handcuffs" on your man it is going to involve some work on your part. The three things you have to work on are making the catch difficult, making them uncomfortable when they do catch the ball and forcing them to their weak side. Your goal should be to make them as uncomfortable as possible so they are taking bad shots or making poor decisions.

The first thing you want to do is make it difficult for them to catch the ball. Since I know you are already in a defensive stance because you have been following the principles I laid out for you, now you want to deny your player the ball. I recognize that In different defensive schemes you might not be denying your player the ball but this is pick-up. So your first goal should be to keep your player from getting the ball at all. You can do this by putting your outside hand in the passing lane and always staying between the ball and your player. Now if you player happens to catch the ball they should be catching the ball at least one step beyond where they wanted the ball. If you are on the perimeter make them go all the way to half court to get the ball! If they are in the post you should make them give up their post position to catch the ball by taking one step to the left or right. I usually front the post and force the opposing team to lob it over the top of me. In general this is a hard pass to make so it leads to turnovers. It is a hard pass to make because they have to pass it over their defender, over me and it has to arrive before my backside help does. I know my teammates are on the midline because they are playing fundamental basketball. So make it difficult for your player to get the ball and they most likely will not even pass them the ball. Your player is now on lockdown!

The second thing you want to do is make it difficult for your player to do what they want to do. Let's say your player does catch the ball. Now you want to concentrate on sliding your feet and staying in front of them but that is a fundamental. The next level is making them uncomfortable. If they have the ball on the perimeter be sure you are pressuring them by mirroring the ball with one hand and using your other hand to stay on balance. Do not be the defender who is just allowing their player to pick apart the defense by not pressuring the passer.

Should your player start to dribble you just want to slide your feet and stay with them. Do not reach! When they pick the ball up again you want to be all over them. If they are in the post then you want to be in a strong defensive stance so they cannot just back you under the basket and score easily. If they have their back to you then be sure to have your forearm in their back. Referees will call fouls in the game if you use your hand but if your forearm is bent you can use it to guide the offensive player away from the basket. Make sure you are not pushing the player. You want to stop them from going where they want to go by using your body as a wall.

The other part about making it difficult on your player is making them take bad shots by forcing them to their weak side. Every player feels more comfortable going one way or the other. Your job is to make them go to their weak side. Notice I said side, not hand. Some right handed people love to be on the left side because they can attack the basket and finish strong with their right, even though it is on the left side. Also you want to be aware of your player's moves and spots. After a couple of plays you should have a pretty good idea of whether your player is a spot up shooter, a slasher or a post player. Make that spot up shooter put the ball on the floor and drive. Make that slasher hit an outside jumpshot. Make that post player catch the ball off the block. Whatever you do, you cannot allow them to do what they do well.

If you do these 3 things together with your fundamentals you will be known as the defensive stopper. You can carry around some handcuffs and hand them out to the player you are guarding because they are locked up!

2) Make plays: Know your opponents and teammates

Observation is the key to any playmaker. To be a playmaker you must be aware of your teammates and your opponents. To be a playmaker it means that you make a play on defense that leads to a stop or on offense that leads to a score.

The first way you can be a playmaker is to be a defensive stopper. Another way you can be a defensive playmaker is to get to the midline. From there you can go block a shot, force a tough shot at the basket or steal a bad pass. If your teammate gets beat make a play by helping them out. If your teammate is in the post getting beasted then go double team so you get the ball out of that player's hands. If you are really paying attention you can shoot the gaps and make a steal or two. You should not attempt to make a play on every possession because if you stick to the fundamentals you will be in good position to get a stop, however there are times when you need to take a chance.

On offense you can be a playmaker in so many ways that do not involve you shooting the ball. Making cuts to the basket are a great way to make plays. If you are open you will get a layup, how easy is that? If you are not open at least you have made the defense move and helped spread the court. Maybe you have a teammate who is great off the dribble but not so great when the help comes. Well if you are moving you can keep your defender from always being the help person. Maybe you have a teammate who is great in the post but keeps getting double teamed by your defender. Move without the ball by cutting or finding a teammate to screen for so they can come to into that post player's vision. If you get your teammate a wide open shot guess what? You just made that play!

If you are a post player one of the best things you can do is pass out of the post. A lot of times you will have a player throw it into the post and then cut to the basket. If your teammate is open hit that player with a nice bounce pass so they can score. Also if you are in the post and you get double teamed you should find the open player and get them the ball so they can score. By being a good post passer you will make the defense hesitate to double you. Now you have one-on-one coverage and the best part is you have the ball where you want it. Enjoy that defender for dinner! If you are on the perimeter see if you can drive through the middle of the court and get somebody to help off their player. If you can do that you will create shots for your teammates. I know we are not keeping stats in a pick-up game but in a real game assists count!

Again this is not about you scoring or getting all of the glory. This is about you making good plays so your team can win.

3) Score: Get to your spot

You should know your game better than anybody else. You know what you do well. You know what you do poorly. In anything you do it is about repeatedly doing what you do well. If you are a brilliant painter then you should have a brush in your hand, paint by your side and an easel in front of you. You should be in your zone. Basketball is no different because we all have our favorite spots to shoot from on the court. Your job should be to get to that spot often and then make a lot of shots from there. So if you are a post player and you really like catching the ball on the right block, you should go to the right block a lot. I am not saying run straight to the block and stand there until you get the ball. You should move around. You could start by setting a screen. Your ultimate goal should be to find a way to get the ball on that right block. Maybe you do this by setting a down screen then sealing your defender on the block. Fantastic now you can tell the defender to enjoy the show! If you are a shooter then you should run off screens all day until you are open for a shot in your favorite spot. I personally love to get the ball in the middle of the floor and shoot mid-range jumpshots. Many of the moves

I make will somehow get me to the middle of the floor. I also love to score in transition so I am always pushing the ball to get an easy shot. You should know right now where you are strong. I will give you a second to think about it. From where do you do the majority of your scoring?

Ok now that you know it is your job to get there. Since you now know where you do the majority of your scoring your job is easy now. You just have to get to those spots and make shots. Simple enough.

4) Pick your move: Unstoppable

Similar to knowing your spot you should know your move. You know what move you make regularly that nobody seems to be able to stop. You should make this move your go to move. Whenever you really need to score you should go to this move. Maybe you have the best drop step in your city, if so you better use it on your defender until they get tired of you scoring so easily. Maybe your crossover leaves defenders with wobbly ankles, you should be cris-crossing your defenders consistently. Maybe you have a shot, well you should be running off screen after screen until you get that open look. Whatever move you feel the most comfortable using, you should use it early and often. This move should be like a freight train barreling down the track: unstoppable.

Just as important as having your unstoppable move is having the counter. The counter to your unstoppable move should be the opposite of your first move. Basketball is much like chess in that you need to see many moves ahead in order to win the game. Having a counter move is necessary because eventually your defender will start to play you to your move. Any smart defender will try to force you to do something different to make you uncomfortable.

As an example let's look at the cross over and the hesitation and how they can work together. When you use the hesitation and go move off the dribble you will have blown by your defender. After a few times of scoring on your defender using the same move eventually they will have to cut you off. That is why you need the crossover. As soon as your defender slides to cut you off that is when you go to the crossover. Now you have your defender thinking they are stopping you from blowing by them and they are just opening the lane the other way for you. You should thank them.

As another example let's look at the pump fake. Let's say you have been catching and shooting on your defender. You have been scoring at will to the point that the other team is getting upset. Now when you catch the ball you will pump fake and your defender will go flying by you. Now you will have a wide open shot. Again you should send some gratitude your defender's way.

This is the mental part of the game that all of the great offensive players play. This is the game within the game. On offense it is all about putting yourself in the best position to score. When you are constantly setting your defender up with a move and a counter move then you will find great success in the scoring column.

5) Be a finisher: Go to guy

"Pressure is a word that is misused in our vocabulary. When you start thinking of pressure, it's because you've started to think of failure."
Tommy Lasorda

The game is to 12 and your team has 11. The other team also has 11. Your team has the ball and the chance to win the game right now on this possession. The defense is getting pumped up, with their vocal leader screaming "We just need 1 stop. 1 stop!" Their scorer has been red hot and knows that if they get a stop they will win the game. As the ball is being dribbled up the court your teammate yells, "I aint going back down to the other end so we better score here." Of all the people on the court, everybody's eyes are glued on you. You make a v-cut to get open. Your teammate makes the pass. You step to the ball, catch it with both hands and square up your defender. No picks are on the way. No double team is on the way. It is you and your defender. What do you do? Well you know that you have been making your jump shot and your defender is a little antsy. You give your defender a hard jab step and they back up a little bit. Now you pump fake hard because your defender is not going to let you just hit the game winning shot them. Whoops your defender should have stayed down, instead they jumped. You take one dribble to the right. Now you have an open shot. You know this is for the game so in your mind you are thinking, do the same thing I always do square up, elevate, arch my shot and follow through. Swoosh! Game time baby, who's got next?

If you have not been in this scenario before then it is time you learn how to be a winner in the clutch. If you find your team needs a big score or a big stop you need to go make a play. In pick-up because the games are so short you have the opportunity to make clutch plays many times throughout the day. If you really want to be a Hooper you have to be able to deliver when the game is on the line. This pick-up game is an opportunity for you to feel a little success and experience a little failure. The more you get comfortable during crucial possessions in a pick-up game the easier it will be to make those plays in your real games. So when it is time here are 9 tips to remember:

1. You have to want the ball
2. You have to have a plan of attack or a go to move
3. You have to be aware of shifts in the defense
4. You have to be aware of open teammates after a defense shifts
5. You have to make the right play and that does not always mean shooting
6. You have to want the ball

7. You have to want the ball
8. You have to want the ball
9. You have to want the ball

Most things in life are all about attitude. So it starts with a desire. In this case you have to want the opportunity to win the game. You have to want the ball. You will build your confidence level tremendously if you just put yourself in pressure packed situations. If you fail so be it but you will learn from it and not make the same mistake next time. Again this is practice, this is where you are supposed to mess up. When you start consistently getting the ball from your teammates and they clear out of your way you know that you have earned the respect and the confidence of your teammates. This will carry over into your season. Your teammates will know they can count on you in the clutch. You will be a Hooper!

Conclusion

"...Every moment you spend on a basketball court should be spent getting better."

Hoops Education, 2012

Since you have read this guide, you have learned a lot of techniques to make sure you are getting the most out of your pick-up games. The biggest thing you want to remember is that every moment you spend on a basketball court should be spent getting better.

You should have a game plan for each pick-up game. I would not recommend trying to do all of these activities at once. I would recommend picking something from each section, Fitness, Fundamentals and Skills, to work on daily. It takes 21 days to form a habit, so after the 21st day you will have incorporated these 3 things into your game. After you have worked on these activities for 21 days or 3 weeks you should assess your progress. Ask yourself, "Have I improved in one of these three categories?" If you have then that is awesome! It is on to the next area. If you have not then you need to revisit what worked, what did not work and potential reasons why you had that outcome. Once you know what went wrong then it is your job to fix it.

Now go start fixing your game so you can be a Hooper!

Hoops Education, 2012

Review

Part 1: Fitness

1. Run
2. Sit down
3. Warm up/Cool down

Part 2: Fundamentals

Defense

1. Box out
2. Challenge shots
3. Slide your feet
4. Get to the midline
5. Get through screens

Offense

6. Use screens
7. Follow your shot
8. Get in triple threat
9. Set screens

Part 3: Skills

1. Become a stopper
2. Make plays
3. Score
4. Pick your move
5. Be a finisher

For more information on how to play basketball, tips and videos sign up for the email list by visiting our website:

hoopseducation.com/email

For bonus material please visit:

hoopseducation.com/howtoplaybasketball

Thanks for reading and for now I'm out!

Hoops Education, 2012

www.ingramcontent.com/pod-product-compliance
Lightning Source LLC
Chambersburg PA
CBHW070204060426
42445CB00032B/1397